Jaya Savige was born in Sydney in 1978 and grew up on Bribie Island. He is a tutor in the School of English, Media Studies and Art History at the University of Queensland, and an arts reviewer for the *Courier-Mail*. He enjoys reading and surfing. He studied English and Philosophy at the University of Queensland, where he received the University Medal for an Honours degree in English in 2001. In 2004 he completed a Master of Philosophy in Creative Writing (UQ). *latecomers* is the winner of the 2004 *Thomas Shapcott Poetry Prize*.

Past Winners of the Arts Queensland
Thomas Shapcott Poetry Prize

2003, *War Is Not the Season for Figs* by Lidija Cvetkovic

latecomers

JAYA SAVIGE

for Lou — have a blast at Byron!

[signature]

UQP

*Singapore —
November 2008*

First published 2005 by University of Queensland Press
PO Box 6042, St Lucia, Queensland 4067 Australia

www.uqp.uq.edu.au

Typeset in 11.5/16pt AGaramond by Post Pre-press Group, Brisbane, Queensland
Printed in Australia by McPherson's Printing Group

Distributed in the USA and Canada by
International Specialized Books Services, Inc.,
5824 N.E. Hassalo Street, Portland, Oregon 97213-3640

 This project has been assisted by
the Commonwealth Government through
the Australia Council, its arts funding
and advisory body.

 Sponsored by the Queensland Office
of Arts and Cultural Development

Acknowledgments

I would like to thank the poetry editors of the following newspapers, magazines, journals and e-zines where these poems have appeared, some in earlier versions:

The Age, Australian Book Review, Big Bridge (USA), *Bribie Weekly, Cordite Poetry Review, The Courier-Mail, Cultural Studies Review, foam:e, GutCult* (USA), *Heat, hutt, Journal of Australian Studies, Meanjin, Overland, papertiger: new world poetry, Poetry Crimes* (*The Red Room Project*), *Retort Magazine, Small Packages, Social Alternatives, Southerly, Stylus Poetry Journal, Unfamiliar Tides* (Newcastle Poetry Prize Anthology 2001/02), *UQ Vanguard* and *The Weekend Australian*.

I am grateful in particular to Bronwyn Lea, David Malouf, Robert Adamson, Laurie Duggan and Martin Duwell for their critical attention, generosity and encouragement. I would also like to thank my family and friends for their ongoing support.

This book of poems was completed with the assistance of an Arts Queensland Literature Grant and a Varuna Writers House Fellowship from the Eleanor Dark Foundation.

in memory of my mother

Contents

III AS THOUGH WE WERE NEVER HERE

when we wake
terrible things have occurred

I

The Unofficial History Pavilion

Desires are already memories

I have come to expect
too much of the ocean.

The tide is out again
researching the month.

Somewhere to the north
lies a heart-shaped reef –

here, a scarab mid-hegira
from its burning island home

clutches in death
a charred Banksia leaf,

bloated and afloat only because
of its legs' grim marriage

with the leaf's serrated edge.
And now I recognise

in its tough, unprisable grip,
the grasp and clutch and grab

and quip of everyone
who's ever known

what it means to not let
go the only thing to come

their way amid the salt scrim
and vicious sprint of the wind.

A union then, with leaves and other
small commuters on the gust

of some apparent consequence;
for, what we seek to hold to

when the world has
loosed its hold on us

may be what prevents us
from never having been.

So the wind discloses
what we cannot relinquish,

even in death, then carries us
from our hearths to foreign beaches,

there to hit upon what each we must,
what it means to be alone, *at last* –

even if only another island in the bay?

Sadness comes in a wave:
the ocean has no stake

in this, betrays no particular desire,
nor any to remember –

perhaps begrudging each our tiny fire.

A place for the rain

here
even the rapids are slow

she crawls through the hollow log
and finds time there

time to handle the fabric of the mountain
time to stitch the moss into couture

there's a place for the rain
behind her eyes –

lightning quickens
in the catchment of her lashes

our breaths commingle, forming a microclimate
no mosquito can fix upon

then, life flashes across our path
in a swift colourful spray

a dragonfly alights upon her hair
I find pause in the thought of her

Odometer

Counting the kilometers
between us.

Tonight you resemble a star:
I see you as you were
many years ago.

Two travellers –
how are they to be as one?

Yet, how far we've come.

Catch you later

I walk towards my shadow
stretched to the end of the street.

The television sells knives.
I hope to convince my siblings

there exists an aeroplane of hope.
They know only stabbed parachutes

and the chortle of the saboteur.
I thought I arrived late, argue this

with my sister: *Is this the face*
that launched a thousand shops?

She matches me for cruelty:
What's that, Shakespeare or something?

Then imagine modern emergency medicos
hacksawing through Marlowe's sternum

to siphon off the excess blood.
My sister's not in the mood

for anachronisms, like *yesterday*
& *now*. So the future it is, with its endless

series of laser-sharpened machetes –
& she, the softest insurgent,

disappears into the night
assuming the bright stars to be blunt.

The partisan

trains, always trains
I can only suppose her death

this frozen landscape
villages filled with gallows

you who sit opposite me
in the same carriage:

will you tear at my flesh
when I am lying in the snow

and you are ravenous?
will your wild eyes forgive me

for having been your comrade?

Souvenir

We arrived as the sun was sinking
into the quicksand of the suburbs.

It seemed everywhere we went
we found a heart in the cement.

We wrenched the bones of day
with pairs of rusty pliers;

they offered almost no resistance:
we ground them down for pigment.

Darkness wrapped each night like a
retaining-wall made of recycled tyres.

The moon was barely a souvenir;
no one could vouch for her existence.

New year's day 1239

It would not do, riding my gaunt horse
To re-enter the world's red dust.

YUAN HAO-WEN (1190–1257)

i.

morning. the artlessness
of half-open apricot blossoms.

so too the image in the mirror changes.

> *great chop of river*
> *refusing allegiance —*
>
> *an angry Yangtze*
> *darkens in the flood*
> *the waking flower.*

ii.

welcome to
the *unofficial history pavilion.*

a dead garden.
the mist, dynasties.

images of geese in the distance
heavy with a hundred smouldering cares.

II

Skirmish Point

Hamartia

They thought our Wirraways were Zeros
our Boomerangs Stuka divebombers
for keeping low as accustomed
during the simulated strafing exercises.
The scaled-down model destroyers' fistfuls
of Oerlikons pumped their percussive punch
& whiz for a whole half hour before they
heard the mayday. I was so deaf
the blood came out like a handkerchief.
Shirl was one of the nurses. I clambered
up the scrambling net of circumstance, as it were,
like I was boarding a mock ship-side.
Everyone said the amphibious exercises at Toorbul
were Churchill's *handling* of the Gallipoli *situation* –
you might then say
had it not been for dad's strife in Turkey,
I may never have met my wife:
the only pure thing to have entered my life.

The master of small violences

He wakes at ten, opens up a can of tinned peaches
and hacks at the succulent halves with a fork taken
from the dish-rack, the only clean utensil left
after a week of neglecting the washing up.
Pushing past split fly-screens in tatters after
making the mistake of feeding next-door's cat,
he flicks some of the syrup at a largish ant crawling
along a frond and four varieties of flies swarm
in like a squadron heeding the sticky reveille.
Some of the syrup hits a spun leaf so that
a spider worries for its sack, stumbles forth,
forelegs raised to attack the assailant, mimicker
of the elements, which it is unable to locate, aimless
in defence. He finds himself inspired each time
a Christmas beetle's wings close incorrectly.
The cat bears gifts: chewed cockroaches beckon
from its jaws. After lunch, ants scamper over crumbs,
march toward a crack, drown, fall off the stainless
splashback. Now the sun's warm paws reach in
through the kitchen window, toying with each web
as at a fraying hem. The sink fills with this predatory
warmth: it is the day drowns them, he is blameless.

Brennan park

I chase the eclipse off the end of the jetty.
The fishermen are all philosophers.
Their nylon beards lean against the sky
like lines of thought the ocean might relate to.
The lorikeets, a truckload of chipped ceramic, tip
into the honey-tide. Here, fate might be a rich nectar,
but Pebble Beach Estate crumbs the mainland horizon,
the type of place one might keep a hammock
in its original plastic. Also, the postman arrives late –
abandoned children snooze in his loading zones.
This to introduce the ghosts of soldiers playing
football in the park across the road to keep fit,
honing the physical tactics of the *parfit*
gentil knight that translate so easily into sport.
To think in life they heard this chorus half
an hour every evening, as I do now;
then found out the hard way history distorts
even the sounds of birds, turns them into scarves
of fire, & the kid fishing into a p.o.w.

Exchange at skirmish point

That which is exchanged should be capable of comparison.
                    ARISTOTLE, 'Nicomachean Ethics'

Elbows raised up above the outgoing tide,
the lead-line of the bait-net is tied around our ankles,
the float-line bobs sedately across the top.
We splash for garfish to sell at our local
tackle-shop, where the news-crew comes
to film the larger flathead for Coastwatch.

Flinders put in for repairs to his starboard
a few hundred yards off a sandbar we call Gilligan's;
confirmed a quantity of pumice on the ebb,
cut open a pine that smelt for all money of turpentine
& stroked the white flowers of the tea-tree.

He swapped the yarn belt that kept him decent
for a fillet made of roo hair; was asked for his hat,
the one with the cabbage tree filaments,
in exchange for her dilly (a bag made of rushes
containing a relative's skin, white clay, red paint,
crude hair comb & a rag for absorbing honey).

He took the dilly, but couldn't relinquish his hat,
& so a spear sailed over the gunwale;
the musket succeeded on the third attempt,
hit one, the rest scattering like buckshot, or
an excess of netted garfish, left chattering on the
  beach.

First avenue

spans the width of the island
connecting the calm of the Passage
to the tiny oceanside suburb, its handful of fish
& chip shops, caravan park, pub and coastal blend
of retirees, lifesavers and young families.

Tonight the message
the roadside wallum bears – despite my fervent wish
that this two-way road stretch
the x light years to Antares, smouldering above
the horizon, not dissimilar to Mars –
the message, then, gestured by the darkening thatch
would be this: that there may be nothing to prove
by cutting the lights, and driving to furthest stars,

unable to keep the secret of this barbed capillary:
that it was forged to shift heavy artillery.

Void if removed
for Nick Drake

circus of light
men fall from the sky

airport blossom of suitcases
which one do you hide in?

you're back from the island
where a tree grows
          up through a car
abandoned during the war

here the months have passed
with each new batch
of baby huntsmen.

The metal detectors

He sang of old coins buried beneath the dunes,
to the north of the island, near the old artillery battery.
For forty years he rowed for mullet north, and south,
where the war-epic motion picture was shot recently.

To the north of the island, near the old artillery battery
we played hide and seek as kids in acres of bladey-grass.
Where the war-epic motion picture was shot recently
no one was allowed within a thousand metres.

We played hide and seek as kids in acres of bladey-grass
behind the northernmost bunker with the stop sign.
No one was allowed within a thousand metres
of the concrete dune, its famed middens of live shells.

Behind the northernmost bunker with the stop sign,
he buried the tin he put his youth in, a stone's throw
from the concrete dune, hidden among the live shells.
I am done trawling, he said. I feared unexploded ordinance.

He buried the tin he put his youth in; the stones knew
about his bushed heart, its unreliable iambs.
I'm done trawling, he said. Then the unexplored co-ordinates,
vast schools flashing before us like escapee payloads

from his bushed heart, its unreliable iambs.
For forty years he rowed for mullet north, and south.
Vast schools flashed before us like escapee payloads
while he sang of old coins, buried beneath the dunes.

Salute the new prospero

whatever you do don't inhale the weapons.
while the antique holocaust breaks over
the head of my tv the terracotta confucius
and plastic robot figurine stand fast.
no point flicking yellow pages
for the broken Ariel, when I know
her to be shackled in the cold
bark of your steel trees, pining
like napalm for children, weeping
waves of radio tears for vile puddles now
huddling on the horizon like stealth bombers.
violet sky over a mosque in Babylon,
I cannot know your fever,
nor the dusty towel of your resolve.
we've but assassins who scamper with cameras
through cribs of crackshot snipers.
the problem is this: I don't think I have
quite the same relationship with death
as you do. not yet anyway . . .
out in the backyard blackhawks flex in circles
preparing for the president. beside the blanket
two ants tussle over a maggot, become
two-headed monster. nearby wasps
with dismembered antennae
attempt to tune in.

Tarpaulin muster

picking up the napkin you articulate my own response
to the rushing noise from beyond the veranda:
'end of the world!' though your father's common sense
provides an alternative to the pregnant pause pricking
the suspense: *'. . . or someone dragging a tarp across the driveway'*
but like the distant sound of a thousand apache helicopters
echoing off the walls of the garage less specific than the thud
of darts or tracers we hear the bullseye pleading
with history like a crater & on the other side
of the world a woman is diagnosed with a rare disease
after the bone dust of a suicide bomber leant
into her own with all the grace of acupuncture.
gather everything now & head for the basement that
isn't even there gather what you need and bid farewell to
summer's shed snakeskins and the kindling you brought
in when it was wet for the earth is soon to be our shelter.
the orchid that split the bark will not be seen
by our children's children, who'll slurp from tins of beans
out of a gash in the container & let the sauce spill
down their chins like insecticide on young strawberries,
their bright grins a mess with the stickiness of necessity.

West end

this gentle aphasia
washes over us like fabric softener.
there's excess
then there's power
autocycling its load
spinning us semi-dry.
the clothesline goes bung.
one of the important strings
has become unstrung
& as the swing-set on the plateau
projects arcs eastward
a stray cat gorges on extra whiskettes.
what are the best odds you can give me
on the west winning back-to-back millennia?
the boundary street festival promises
to be the most memorable yet.

National museum

a currawong pecks at scraps
but looks at me askance.

my sunglasses slip
onto my nose
from off my apparently polemical
gallery of hair – the bird becomes suspicious.

across the lake
parliament house peers through
the crisp monocle of the capital.

the tactical colours of a
yacht club sway in figdark water
darker than a tea-tree bay.

the pupil as a basin
& I'm sucked into the lens,

      sucked into the nest,
      sucked into the cataract of the civic.

the wide eye glazes over,
a thin, darkening film.

Halfmast

The one day of the year & I forget
how to tie the knot that once kept up appearances,
                    or at least kept them halfway up.

The afternoon sun is prone
                    the way a young chaplain
sailing in a duck-boat up the Dardenelles,
past ancient Troy,
                    might have knelt before the lord.

Out on the veranda sandflies react to a focus
            as if nan's knitting needles
                    worked by themselves for a tea-cosy
I might one day use as a beanie.

There's John in the background:
            . . . *if yr lonely you c'n talk to me* . . .
                    & though his altruism is a nice token
something tells me he isn't really listening.

Come in under the shade of this sports-betting ledge, John

& suddenly I forget who it is I'm talking to.
So an audience forgets, as soon as it's forgotten.

Yr fly's undone, remarks the drunk
at the Story Bridge Hotel.

At least I can do that up.

Settlement

beyond the bay window
a jumble of undulant breasts.

gym bunnies stretch muscles
I've never heard of, surfers fetch

the swell as it comes and goes in sets
like the gaudy fort da game of cigarettes.

bombs on the front page.
the tractor almost runs over us,

our arse-prints leavening the serious
sand, wanting a rake for tourism

& the temporary tattoo
of our national flag

is taking days to disappear
off the back of my hand.

The stairs at epidaurus

In the case of salt-water pools that meet the ocean
the split between the two is often indistinct.

I went to the store for tonic, came back with ginger ale –
these small cracks pertain to diffusive futures, so take

two steps for the height of every barricade to make it.
Stroll with the ritual simplicity of a spiral minaret

but in the case of a sixteen piece stoneware dinner set
remember tiny portions leave a frame for our perspective.

When designing bridges or boiling the jug for coffee, think
De Chirico was not Dutch; neither was Mark Rothko.

Note that natural light alone chastens the chapel of Ronchamp,
that both the stark architecture of a Cistercian church

and the spiral jetty know that they themselves are pointless,
going nowhere in particular – though they stop to see us

try to keep our word and quit our own impassive orbit.
Ten feet. Feels good. Stand-by for touchdown on two.

Satellite dishes want humble forms to show themselves
less so, as if sensual figures were set against a measured

grid, but the elemental arts corrode our robust patios
and ruthlessness is just a silhouette, the perfect zig-zag

of a bomber for example, or the basic vision of cutlery,
quite the chase of Bach on the piano –

the endless fugue of culture arrives like so many waves,
an unlit set that tilts the balance, until, too deep

for us to stand, it gathers like the clouds of swollen
storms that threaten sullen swimmers with their

silent lightning, a code, perhaps, deciphering itself
to pure darkness.

Marginal propensity

a. the new paganism

save!   new range antiperspirant apollo   (you pay less!)
        inca & gravity   justright / ironman flies by   flybuys explosion!
        fine grade mince   two kilogram minimum buy
                    mars   snickers   (save . . .)

b. the new monotheism

save!   radiant ultraconcentrate dynamo   birdseye (original)
        dollar dazzler / sunsilk maximum shine   original vanilla
        original flora . . . new improved mainland variety

i. youth

save! high performance fruit salad rainbow
for baby! chicken-in-a-biscuit (great value!)
natural confectionery party animals

ii. middle age

save! energizer max? acme smokealarm
plenitude turning point (huge savings)
straight chips twenty percent free

iii. retirement

save! pedigree pal!
your one chance to

win! freedom!
(furniture)

The captain wish bridge

Negligence: not the rare forgetfulness
of she who answers the door

in her underwear. No. But the wind
as it toys with a sheet of aluminium

tied down too loosely on a tradesman's tray.
Local traffic slows to merge onto the highway.

The Landrover full of children swerves
to miss it, the cattle stand oblivious to the skid.

The elderly man in the old Toyota
as though the windshield were a mouth

and he, the soft tongue cut
unkindly, an innocent convicted

by the wind of being a cold war spy,
silenced by the keenest prosecution.

I cross this bridge up to ten times a week,
and each time dwell on the futility

of surviving all the death the world has
to offer, when a fellow man's negligence

can end it all so swiftly, at eighty!
Indeed the bridge compels me now to wish

that the carelessness that leads
to tragedies like these never be mine,

and that if my lover lives that long,
they not be snatched in such a way as this.

Piscosos scopulos

Spring arrived like a car-accident outside a hospital.
I retched upon the golf shoes of Hippocrates.

Then the archaeology: finding my bearings
not in the bronze likeness on the lawn entrance

to the medical college, but in the sounds of the rock
concert jagging off the adjacent children's hospital.

At some stage during the night
the sole of my shoe had come loose:

the floppy thong slapped upon the pavement
like Virgil's 'rocks teeming with fish' –

     'PI-SCO-SO-S SCO-PU-LOS' –

as dawn, in lieu of a leather sandal,
burst into another of its tropical brass buckles.

Directions

To get there: leave the Sea of Rains & head southwest
for *Oceanus Procellarum*, the Ocean of Storms —
then inland sharply to Copernicus, an eleven thousand
foot tall impact crater. Light catches off its lip
with a twelve and a half mm eyepiece.
Notice Delaunay to the south, then due east across
the Sea of Vapors, near to Julius Caesar,
Descartes now to the south. Allow the eye to
rest in the gentle darkness of *Mare Tranquilitatis*.
Northeast you'll see the Sea of Crises, difficult to ignore,
it makes the moon look like the deathstar.
Then, fifty degrees south, seventy degrees east,
near to *Mare Australe*: an almost unnoticeable crater
named Brisbane.

Neomenia

with the moon behind us, we might begin again
in its absence constellations slough their unfair curfew
& bite their brightening thumbs behind its back
warm farrago, cheeky retinue of the icy phoenix

in whose absence constellations slough their unfair curfew
& so our spangled tomb, its must lyrical with rebirth
warm farrago, cheeky retinue of the icy phoenix
that rises from its periodic char, reappears after its taper

& so our spangled tomb, its must lyrical with rebirth
in this pause to suffer hope's intolerable burden
that rises from its periodic char, reappears after its taper
when spectres of possibility ambuscade the sepulchre

in this pause we suffer hope's intolerable burden
the scent of reincarnation, waft of effluvial paraffin
when spectres of possibility ambuscade the sepulchre
and albums of dust cozen auroras of calendars

cement of reincarnation, soft, of effluvial paraffin
from which history's angel fashions its own image
as albums of dust cozen auroras of calendars
and each breath proves the impulse of a palimpsest

from which history's angel fashions its own image
we bite our brightening thumbs behind its back
and each breath proves the impulse of a palimpsest
with the moon behind us, we might begin again

Flyer (Autumn)

I take great mouthfuls of the fresher air –
Autumn, in the back of my throat.
An icy renaissance races across my arms,
hands and face, and any other part
of my body exposed to the new season.
Your eyelashes too have become colder;
when we kiss I feel one touch my cheek,
an elegant fan of the thinnest icicles
that might not melt until the coming spring.
Here a flyer in the gutter gets a little bolder
then finally takes off again down Roma Street,
lifting its shoulders, donning a new suit,
overcome by imminent possibility.

III

As Though We Were
Never Here

Mercedes

she says her mother will kill her
she asks for a cigarette

not for me she says *don't smoke . . .*
my mother will kill me . . . but do you
have a cigarette for my mother?

she smokes the cigarette
returns with a handful of ashes

i don't understand what she's asking of me
i tell her to throw them in the gutter

she says she's an island girl
& asks if i have seen her mother

i'm stuck somehow on the *Mercedes* –
latin for *reward* – boasting by the curb

she says again she doesn't smoke
but her mother smokes
she's trying to find her mother

she asks for a cigarette
she says her mother will kill her

The famous pitch drop experiment

scientia ac labore

I try to distinguish the physics foyer in the twilight
When the fleeting sandstone lintels appear identical
An average interval has passed since I was here
Even now the sable pitch succumbs

The fleeting sandstone lintels appear identical
Within: a deadly black bird, nesting in a glass funnel
Even now the sable pitch becomes
Proof pending of interminable autumn

Within: a deadly black bird, nesting in a glass funnel
Then in death our breath becomes absurd
Proof pending of interminable autumn
Ten billion times more viscous than the ocean

Then in death your breath became a bird
When your breast stopped; only mine returned
Ten billion times more vicious than devotion
Imperceptible, mute conundrum of the hours

Had the drip stopped? Was time spurned?
An average interval has passed since I was here
Imperceptible, mute conundrum of the hours –
I try to distinguish the physics from you in the twilight

Wake

like the poet
(always running late)

death wears
whatever is at hand

To the river, burning

In hindsight her backache
was the suffering of Andromache.

Dawn bludgeons its hegemonic pax:
I over-balance, an everyday Astyanax,

& these all-too-expensive nicotine
patches recall the earlier St. Augustine.

It is not my place to mother
my siblings, but it's another

humid summer, and school's the last
thing on their minds. Over breakfast

I divine that the missing feathers of Archaeopteryx
were smoked on time's black market; and that Styx

runs underneath all rivers, *Yangtze, Ganges, Euphrates* . . .
for I row upon the paperchain this Hades incinerates.

Mandarin

I separate the seeds from a mandarin
using my tongue and teeth together.
Sun-emblazoned tambourine.

Then consider the endeavour of those
microscopic creatures that must
eat their way out of their own mother.

Or are they blessed who must erase
all trace of their past to gain passage
into this dust?
                  They'd never question

whether they discovered enough
before her last, about themselves,
about herself, and the way the world

thought when she was just a tot.
Nor would they remember how
she burst in selfless ecstasy

just as they were done dining.
Perhaps it's the ease with which
I spit these seeds into the bin.

Nothing will come of them.

Infrared madonna

by the strange dance
    of a rocky outcrop

an x-ray saint feels
    the surface pinch –

awkward foreshortening
    in the attachment of wings.

by the strange dance
    of a rocky outcrop

we are as pregnant women
    craving things we've never

particularly cared for
    probably abhorred.

see how the star flares up
    relieved of its occultation;

the mother as a twin then
    and the twin a revelation –

over every saint's shoulder
        an infrared Madonna!

(her torsion nothing short
        of Whiteley's priapic blues)

Currency lad

Darwin, four years before I am born
         & your perm
is an informant for Cyclone Tracy.

The way you'd pirouette into an Arnhem bar
         like an exotic cocktail
         no-one's ever thought to order.

Further south you took an Indonesian lover
& left him windswept,
         beguiled by your gyre.

I cannot remember
whether you said he was a

        a)   boatperson
        b)   philanthropic businessman
               who sold drapery in Glebe or
        c)   free-wheeling drug-dealer
               with little other expertise.

This afternoon outside my window
implausible plastic fencing
prevents traipsing on an imported lawn.

The mud is heavy underfoot.
A swift spring wind toots through the court
like an army of tin roofs routed.

Since you left for that place
far beyond Perth,

     I've found myself buried
     in a study

     of swamp drainage
     & mosquito birth,

where the harsh susurrus of skulls,
the sough of each gaping eye-socket,
accuses the composite silences of my marsh,

     the way loose change shouts
     from my otherwise empty pocket.

Agapanthus/letter to martin johnston
i.m. D.S.

i

an agapanthus petal   slams into a whirlpool
         Eli / to attain cold peace but / *Eli*
the cross oxygen makes ice-cream sear cognisance / *lama sabachthani*
hard into the sacrificial chicane or morphine corridor
        where the incest of Hypnos & Thanatos
         attends spines with scalding shovels.

agapanthus means 'flower of love'
not this inert filigree of tactile silence
never thought I'd slow you down this much –
you were young in Sydney a bowl & I
the swollen oats a stone a heavy lump so there you lie

now in the smithy of the Pacific to test a new cocktail
the 'H-Bomb' (for horizon) / paracetamol plus scotch for dusk
& the stars rattle along to Bikini Atoll (radiant for fashion in France
posing as a cryptic clue) but   all the stars are falling here
alone in the close between the chapel & you

Magellan sarong of Venus wrapped twice around that
year we scaled: the fibreglass simulacrum
                        of a Glasshouse Mountain

you crossed the passage on a ski
left me to fumble this frothy umbel of darkening seas

the beach a breakfast of wild honey & I'm stuck
at the stall of dawn, some lone golden fruit tumbling
in reverse, up from behind a broken island cart

squinting at the atrocity of this luminous cyclonic corona
lifting itself up on its taut right shoulder

                        there is silence for a time
                        after each wave crashes

a frail palliative shawl drapes her bluebottle waterfall
(some jellies you can throw as discs)
the moon has poured out all her vinegar &

the intercontinental ballistic missile of rhythm shatters
the catch: the frequency of myth
with each sharp breath / myth of sequent toil a set of stills

iii

so I sit to write 'still life with cigarette' like a
near-sighted comedian with a far-out tragic joke
or an argument over religion without the safety of a text
but   I cannot fill the void between now & what comes next

then bump into *tableaux vivants*:

random newspaper pentameter –
SERIAL RAPIST FAINTS AT GUILTY VERDICT

& we are back with Ovid (for psychoanalysis):
the Actheon press corrodes the swift mercedes
possesses Diana in a net of steel chassis

Coemus! . . . Coemus!
reflection the frieze of recognition
iste ego sum: sensi nec me mea fallit imago . . .

foetal mirror of mercury so poisonous
your pancreas burst for these truly dismal baptisms

so I ask can the somnolent planet of
metempsychosis divert our dark itinerary?

if not then skip to
nautical prodigy sketching empty coastlines
with recent model sextant for this whirlpool of death

Athena, make haste to help me for I twitch like your son
an Odyssean sea cucumber thumb
become numb rusk of a deep-sea cowboy at high noon-tide –

        charting the distance from
        Persephone to Proserpina –

her dark eyes avenge her smudged mascara
the guard checks that the chapel doors are locked.

Sunshine coast exit

you walk into a room
she has died

he is dying
it is the same room

Free to air

Nightfall – flat coke
in the bottom of the bottle.

I hunt events with
the remote control,

knowing
it is always another
that makes this moment possible.

Jemimah, dove

Light rain drizzles through
small holes in the pergola gauze
onto the open diary.

We wheel-in your damp pram.
Evening baffles you with its elephant steps:
grave humps of apocalyptic timpani

or the future as a boeing jumbo
that flies low over the garden
once every three or four minutes.

No panic in the fruit bat though
in its jaws we witness the seed's failure.
Again those metal pteradons

terrorise mum's rented property.
Your gingerbread becomes
a prop in the terrible opera,

& you, the chubby soprano,
whose ascendant aria renders each
hijacked *lufthansa* insignificant.

Serein

the tumuli of you
& these dunes

your lips twin pumices
your smile exfoliates my skin

the beacons in the bay converse
silent baskets of information

snakecharmers kiss
blind the horizon

& we are part of the petrichor
forever in the non-arrival

(or late like a pallet of pastels
to a pre-Raphaelite ball)

our bodies wring the air & spike
the punch with lightning mango

your footprints the dapple
of the rain-packed sand

Poem

the heart
a bird of stone

a masterpiece reproduced
on a postage stamp

in the jaws of a fifty foot wave

A place for the rain II

afternoons
raincoating through waterfalls

vagaries of light   she accidentally
photographs a rainbow

her eyes bioluminesce
daytime constellations

her tongue, tentative bird
confides in our nest of lips

my skin exceeds awareness
but is more ecstatic

than the plastic bag
amid the strangler figs

I think of the symbiosis
between trapdoors and glowworms

either way I mistranslate
the aspect of her soul

Now that no one is watching

another beautiful day –

        palm fronds nod on the breeze
        a wasp bounces by a rusted support

even the sound of a truck stuck in second
bound for a timber quarry on the Sunshine Coast
hauling its load
                  goads the quiet
the way a salt poultice draws wine from the carpet.

a box of matches from the Monastery (nightclub)
a two-tiered ashtray
      both layers the iconic shape of flowers.

you enter
exhausted from singing & dancing 'I go to Rio'

proceed to show me a new swivel of the hips
that you couldn't do in class but
can now that no one is watching but me.

Silent night

Bottle-top trivia masses on the lawn.
After backyard cricket it's the garden hose
versus water-bombs and water-pistols.
These summer antics! You take a piece
of ice from the esky, then slip it down
the top of someone you're attracted to.
                    But now the day is done,
the paper plates all cleared away,
the children, having chased all afternoon,
exhausted and asleep on grandma's couch –
now the cd that was on repeat has ceased –
we are left with this: the evening's stillness,
beyond the flutter of the tarp, a kind of peace
between us, a late gift we give to each other
in silence, so complete, so unexpected.

Fast asleep

i

night
that black wasp

my dream
a cross between

the sting
and the proboscis

ii

evening languorous as
the eyelid of a tired Cyclops

rush past often clutching
abdomens of feeble sheep

get stuck spelunking in a bog
the eye becomes a delicacy

The light works, turn it on

A dark road.
At this, you break up. It's only
the thin bisque of oblivion.
The light works, turn it on. You're asleep,
how can you be speaking? *So much death,* your hand
over your heart, *so much death – and men
in Chinese soup.* You climb the ladder
of the dream, then raise the lid,
and all you have to do is sing.

Paramedic

Under the new moon, vehicles in the distance
lose their way and bawl their grief aloud.
To the rescue, the banshees of the ambulance
ululate, their desperate shroud . . .

Sirens slam shut apertures of silence
Rain falls slow as glass
The windscreen a shower of scalpels
The concept of sharpness must involve angles

Rain falls slow as glass
Centuries pass before the storm hits
The concept of sharpness must involve angles
Angles are contrary to the human body

Sentries pass before the storm hits
The guards of my flesh forgetting how soft it is
Angels are contrary to the human body
Can-openers keen only to get a can's contents

The guards of my flesh forgetting how soft it is
The windscreen a flower of scalpels
Can-openers keen only to get a can's contents
Sirens commence their overture of violence

Investment

I dare you to buy
someone's art

then murder them
so the price goes up

The dreamworld murders

I

If you like
I will take you to him.

The moment I saw
his body on the news,

I suspected myself of murder.

I will take you to the swamp
with the concrete blocks,

along the bmx track
dogs chase your bike down,

and show you the black water
where his face sings still.

II

Who funded these tunnels?
Who cut these stairs into the cliff face?

And where would all the water
go without these weirs?

She is heavy in this water.
She is heavy on these stairs.

III

Step with me into the massacre
of shadows, my carport, where

thick sweaty ogres of darkness
elbow unremittingly.

I caught you earlier, prostrate
before the matron of the moon.

I overheard you asking to be spared.

Step with me into the car
and I shall spare you.

IV

Spiders camp
in her mouth.

Time's bride yawning
in her wedding webs.

Roll her over to see
the young feed on her spine.

What flame through the enfilade?
Hurry, someone approaches!

Put things back the way they were!

It must appear as though
we were never here . . .

V   (death by naming)

Behind the brick wall a dead tree
whose leaves are hundreds
of vagrant butterflies.

This then is the wardrobe
where the darkness begins,

74

and out there are the many things
the summer day discloses, things

the light touches and lends
existence to. Herein I hold your name

the way a spider tends
an exhausted glasswing,

but it slips from my web
and shatters on the cement

into a thousand tiny eulogies.

VI

I swear the weapon
is around here somewhere,

deep in the burgeoning suburb of the past.
I intend to spend my last days here, fossicking.

Only the rumour of the ocean,
its dark unsolvable crime,

and the sky littered with clues
that corroborate my alibi.

VII

I have been weak,
but now my strength returns.

Someone else's comics
in the letterbox –

planes blink in place
of correspondence.

In the red house across the road:
a family of raw meat.

There the world's last
sidekick lies unconscious.

VIII

One by one you killed-off
all your fathers.

The flexibility of bamboo –
you choose to wear no uniform.

A small faceless
animal faces me.

A corpse in loose cerements on
the back seat of the getaway car

IX

Pastures of nightshade.
The rain's faint pulse.

The pain of knowing objects fades –
in the end we do not need them.

X

Death is in the bone
the wind picks with the leaves.

You've come so far
to discover all this

could be blown away
in one unimaginable gust.

Time becomes
a simple case of being

backed-up against the wall of death,
an indefinite series of last chances.

Death comes soon enough
which must be worse –

for then one's forced to say that
yes, they were lost

who did not know their way
among the vanishing.

Sky

stabbed twenty-six times
left naked as the afternoon
in the dense understorey
of a swale bladey-grassed
depression imposing as
the lair of your lassitude
weapons experts mope
about the shallow pools the
ocean cramps with growing
pains dumps its fireweed
burning in a bush of wave
& composure is a mottled
turtle swimming close
to the rough surface
of the sea —

Intercession

sitting on the back steps and it is
a basketball hoop without a net   appearing like a halo
above an empty garage   the taste of ashes or
any avalanche of all the one flavour mesmerising
the asphalt screen of a television set   using the hoop
as an aerial for us to wonder at these ashes in colour
so prayer remains the cheapest psychoanalysis
& the keys to this duplicity (the cars of two lovers
locked together in a multi-storied carpark) are an aria
in the opera of a thief's pockets   about a woman
who scrapes hardened gum off footpaths & watches
feet burn on the tar in summer   waiting for a steamroller
to send her home early   over by the escalator
a melted button becomes her stubborn shrine

Notes

The epigraph is from Michael Dransfield's poem 'Couplets'.

Desires are already memories. The title is a phrase from Calvino's *Invisible Cities.*

Brennan park. The italicised phrase 'parfit gentil knight' is from 'The General Prologue' to Chaucer's *Canterbury Tales.*

Piscosos scopulos. The title is a phrase from Virgil's *Aeneid* (4. 255). It can be translated as 'Rocks teeming with fish'.

Agapanthus / letter to martin johnston. '*Eli, Eli, lama sabachthani*' is translated from the Aramaic as 'My God, my God, why hast thou forsaken me?' (Matt. 24:46). '*Coemus!* . . . *Coemus!*' (Let us meet! . . . Let us meet!) is from Ovid's *Metamorphoses* (III. 463). Narcissus says *Iste ego sum: sensi, nec me mea fallit imago* (O, I am he! I have felt it, I now know my own image) when he recognises his reflection.